SPIES OF
THE CIVIL WAR

AN INTERACTIVE HISTORY ADVENTURE

by Michael Burgan

Consultant:
Malcolm J. Rohrbough, PhD
Professor Emeritus, Department of History
The University of Iowa

CAPSTONE PRESS
a capstone imprint

You Choose Books are published by Capstone Press,
1710 Roe Crest Drive, North Mankato, Minnesota 56003
www.capstonepub.com

Library of Congress Cataloging-in-Publication Data
Burgan, Michael.
Spies of the Civil War : an interactive history adventure / by Michael Burgan.
pages cm.—(You choose: spies)
Includes bibliographical references and index.
Summary: "Explores various perspectives on espionage in the Civil War. The reader's
choices reveal the historical details"—Provided by publisher.
Audience: Grade 4 to 6.
ISBN 978-1-4914-5859-4 (library binding)
ISBN 978-1-4914-5932-4 (pbk.)
ISBN 978-1-4914-5944-7 (ebook)
1. United States—History—Civil War, 1861-1865—Secret service—Juvenile
literature. 2. Espionage—United States—History—19th century—Juvenile literature.
3. Spies—United States—History—19th century—Juvenile literature. I. Title.
E608.B88 2015
973.7'85—dc23   2015010896

Editorial Credits
Adrian Vigliano, editor; Ted Williams, designer; Kelly Garvin, media researcher

Photo Credits
Getty Images: Buyenlarge, 58, Education Images, 32, Kean Collection, 35, 103, MPI,
62, 90, Print Collector, 49; Granger, NYC, 16, 53, 69, 85, 99; National Archives and
Records Administration, cover, 1; Library of Congress: Brady-Handy Photograph
Collection, 40, Civil War Photograph Collection, 20, 26, Prints and Photographs
Division, 6, 12, 24, 70, 100, 105; North Wind Picture Archives, 10, 77

Printed in Canada
032015   008825FRF15

TABLE OF
CONTENTS

4

ABOUT YOUR ADVENTURE

You are living through America's massive Civil War. You have chosen to join in the fight as a spy. That means using secret codes, wearing disguises, gathering information—and trying not to get caught.

In this book you'll explore how the choices people made meant the difference between life and death. The events you'll experience happened to real people.

Chapter One sets the scene. Then you choose which path to read. Follow the directions at the bottom of each page. The choices you make will change your outcome. After you finish your path, go back and read the others for new perspectives and more adventures.

YOU CHOOSE the path you take through history.

CHAPTER 1

WAR DIVIDES THE UNITED STATES

You are living in the United States in the spring of 1861. Fighting has broken out between Northern and Southern states over slavery and the rights of states to make their own laws.

Abraham Lincoln was elected president in November 1860. Before he was elected, he supported keeping slavery out of new U.S. territories and states. But as president, he said he would allow slavery to exist where it had for years.

7

TURN THE PAGE.

Owners of African-American slaves didn't trust Lincoln to protect slavery in the South. That was one reason 11 Southern states seceded from the Union beginning in 1860 and into 1861. They formed their own nation, the Confederate States of America.

Lincoln believes the Southern states have no right to secede. He recently called for 75,000 volunteers to fight the Confederacy. The Confederacy is determined to fight for its independence. The nation is now involved in a civil war.

At the start of the war, the U.S. military didn't have a spy agency. But Lincoln sees espionage as a way to learn the enemy's plans. Confederate leaders also consider spying important.

When it comes to spying, the Confederacy has several advantages. Many Southerners work for the Union government in Washington, D.C. Those supporting the Confederacy can keep their views secret and keep their jobs. They can then gather information to pass to Southern leaders.

TURN THE PAGE.

Citizens of Charleston, South Carolina, watch the Civil War begin on April 12, 1861, as Confederates fire on the Union's Fort Sumter.

The Union doesn't have a similar ability to collect information in the Confederate capital of Richmond, Virginia. Also, four slave states—Delaware, Maryland, Kentucky, and Missouri—remain in the Union. Some people in these border states support the Confederacy. Confederate spies working in the North can count on them for help. Fewer Southerners support the Union, so Northern spies working in the South cannot count on much help.

Both sides are building networks of spies. You decide to join them. You know the importance of learning what the enemy plans to do. But you also understand you risk prison or execution if you are caught.

11

TO BE A DETECTIVE SPYING FOR THE UNION, TURN TO PAGE 13.

TO BE A SOUTHERN WOMAN SPYING FOR THE CONFEDERACY, TURN TO PAGE 41.

TO BE A FREE BLACK MAN SPYING FOR THE UNION, TURN TO PAGE 71.

Allan Pinkerton was chief of intelligence for Union General George McClellan during the Civil War.

CHAPTER 2

DETECTIVE FOR THE UNION

"You did good work back in February. Now I have another important job for you."

You listen to your boss, Allan Pinkerton, the founder of a famous Chicago detective agency. In February 1861 you and other Pinkerton detectives learned of a Confederate plot to kill President-elect Lincoln as he traveled through Baltimore, Maryland. Thanks to your group, Lincoln safely reached Washington, D.C.

13

You enjoy being a detective. It was the first job you took after moving to the United States from England five years ago. Now you're curious about the new job Pinkerton has for you.

TURN THE PAGE.

"General George McClellan wants my detectives to spy on the Confederacy."

"I'm ready," you say. You want to help the Union stay together.

Pinkerton explains that he has several missions. He needs someone to join a secret group in Baltimore called the Knights of Liberty. Its members want Maryland to secede from the Union. They are stirring up violence in Baltimore. Pinkerton also needs someone to travel through the border states.

"We need to know what Southern troops are doing in those areas," Pinkerton explains. "And we want to know which Northerners might try to help them if they invade us. Which job would you like?"

14

TO GO TO BALTIMORE,
GO TO PAGE 15.

TO TRAVEL ALONG THE BORDER,
TURN TO PAGE 23.

You take a train to Baltimore. You rent a room there and call yourself Jacob Smith. You tell people that you came from England to start a clothing business, and you support the Confederacy. Over time you meet a number of men who belong to the Knights of Liberty. They aren't sure if they can trust you at first. But you convince them that you want to help Maryland secede.

Some of the leading Knights members want to go to Richmond, the capital of Virginia. They fear they could be arrested if they stay in Baltimore. You know they will be arrested— because you're telling Pinkerton about their plans. One member, William Cooper, wants you to come to Richmond too.

TURN THE PAGE.

"We're not safe here," he says. "I'm sure there must be Union spies around."

You have important work to do in Baltimore. But you might be able to do some useful spying in Richmond. Traveling with the Knights will convince Confederate officials that you can be trusted.

The Stars and Stripes of the Union flies in Baltimore in May 1861. On April 19 Confederate supporters had rioted against Union troops.

TO STAY IN BALTIMORE, GO TO PAGE 17.

TO GO TO RICHMOND, TURN TO PAGE 19.

"I have business here in Baltimore for a week," you tell Cooper. "Maybe I'll join you later."

You spend the next few days traveling to Washington and meeting with Pinkerton. Back in Baltimore, you eat dinner at a restaurant with several Knights. Another Knight, Jesse Douglas, approaches the table. He strides up to you with an angry look on his face.

"Smith, who are you?"

"What do you mean?" you ask, trying to stay calm.

"Is that your real name?" Douglas says, pulling you to your feet. "I think you're a spy! I saw you in Washington the other day."

"I haven't left Baltimore in weeks," you say. "Maybe you saw someone who looked like me."

17

TURN THE PAGE.

"You were hanging around government buildings," Douglas snaps. "You're a Union spy."

"How dare you accuse me!" you shout as you push him away. Douglas comes back at you with a knife in his hand. You pull a small gun from your coat pocket and point it at him.

"I am not a spy, and I will not let you ruin my honor with that kind of talk," you say. "I support the South, just as we all do." Douglas stares at you coldly. He puts down his knife and stomps out of the restaurant. Your heart pounds as the other Knights applaud your courage. You were just reminded of how dangerous spying can be. But you're not going to stop. Maybe it's time to go to Richmond.

18

GO TO PAGE 19.

You tell Pinkerton about your new plan.

"That's a good idea," he says. "We won't arrest the men traveling with you. But there are some other Confederate supporters in Baltimore we can nab— including the mayor."

The next day Cooper, you, and several other Knights leave for Virginia. Confederate leaders welcome you as you arrive in Richmond.

You get to know people in the Confederate government. You meet military officers too. They allow you to visit some battlefields outside the city. You note the location and strength of Confederate forces. Military officers allow you to pass as you travel back to Baltimore with a local Confederate merchant.

As Confederate General Raymond Johnson lets you pass through, he asks for a favor.

TURN THE PAGE.

"We have spies in Washington," he says. "You can safely travel there since you're from Maryland. Could you bring information to them and bring back messages they have for us?"

You realize that this would make you a double agent! Working for Johnson, you might be able to get even more important information for Pinkerton. But you will face extra pressure pretending to work for the Confederates.

a group of Confederate Secret Service agents in Virginia

TO HELP JOHNSON,
GO TO PAGE 21.

TO REFUSE, TURN TO PAGE 31.

You take a packet of information from Johnson and continue traveling to Maryland and then to Washington, D.C. Before you give Johnson's letters to the Confederate spies, you visit Pinkerton. He copies the information.

"After you give these to the spies," Pinkerton says, "bring me any information they have for the Confederate military. We'll make sure you don't deliver anything useful to the South. But we'll include some of the information so they'll trust you and not suspect you're a double agent."

For several months, you travel freely between Richmond and Washington. You carry useful information to Pinkerton. Meanwhile, the Confederates get only a few small details about Union troop movements.

TURN THE PAGE.

On one trip back to Virginia, you take a ferry across the Potomac River. Also on the ferry are a Southern woman, Jane, and her daughter, Sarah. The boat is anchored a short distance from the shore. You offer to carry Jane and Sarah through the water to the ferry. You're soaked to your waist. You reach Virginia safely. But within a few days, you come down with a fever and a hacking cough. In Richmond you meet up with Joe Scully, another Union spy working in the city.

"You look terrible," Joe says. "Maybe I should make the next trip north for you."

You feel terrible. Wading through the cold river water must have weakened you. But you're not sure Joe should go. He doesn't know all of your contacts on the way to Maryland.

22

TO MAKE THE TRIP,
TURN TO PAGE 27.

TO STAY IN RICHMOND,
TURN TO PAGE 29.

You board a train to Cincinnati, Ohio. From there, you travel to the Confederate city of Memphis, Tennessee. You introduce yourself as Jonathan Sewell, a Baltimore businessman and strong supporter of the South.

As you talk with people, you casually ask about friends and relatives who are fighting for the Confederacy. They tell you about them and the armies they serve. You also see troops outside the city and learn what you can about where they're going. Your new friends introduce you to the officers, and they tell you even more information. You prepare a report to mail to Pinkerton once you reach Ohio, a Union state.

23

Memphis residents have recently created a safety committee to catch Northern spies who come to the city. The committee carefully watches any stranger who comes to town.

TURN THE PAGE.

"We should hang any blasted Yankee that tries to spy here," one man says.

You join the crowd in agreeing with him. But you know you'll have to be even more careful now that the committee is keeping an eye on newcomers. It might be better to leave Memphis and continue traveling through Tennessee.

Spying on army camps could provide useful information about the enemy's numbers, strength, and movement.

TO STAY IN MEMPHIS,
GO TO PAGE 25.

TO LEAVE MEMPHIS,
TURN TO PAGE 34.

24

Pinkerton stressed the importance of getting information in Memphis, and that's what you'll do. You spend the day with a new friend, Dr. David Burns. He once lived in Baltimore, so you have something in common. He takes you to a nearby army camp to meet some Confederate officers. When you return, you see a man hanging around outside your hotel. He wears a dark, wide hat that partly hides his face.

The next day you head to the station to board a train for Chattanooga, Tennessee. You notice the same man in the hat and another man close behind you. You get on your train, which is packed with soldiers. You can't see if the men followed you. At the first stop, you leave that train and quickly board another. Now you see the two men leave the first train and enter yours. They're following you!

25

TURN THE PAGE.

You get off at the next stop and board a third train. The two men do the same and take a seat in the rear of your car. You start to sweat. The men must be waiting to follow you off the train to arrest you. Should you confront them? You're confident that they can't prove you're a spy. But it might be safer to try to lose them at the next stop of Humboldt.

Thousands of miles of railroad track had been laid in Northern and Southern states in the 1850s. Railroads became an important method of transportation for both sides in the war.

TO CONFRONT THE MEN, TURN TO PAGE 36.

TO TRY TO LOSE THEM, TURN TO PAGE 38.

"I'm fine, Joe," you say. "I'll go."

You gather information for several days. One night Joe comes to your room.

"We're in trouble," he says. "The rebels arrested John Ferris."

Your eyes widen. Ferris is another Union spy working in Richmond.

"They were going to hang him," Joe continues, "until he told them the names of every Northern spy he knew."

"Did he mention us?" you ask.

"I don't know, but we can't take a chance. We need to leave now."

You still feel sick, but you know Joe is right.

"We have to be careful," you say. "The police will arrest anyone out after the curfew."

TURN THE PAGE.

"I know where we can get horses," Joe says. "If we can reach them, we should be all right."

You hide the information you've gathered under a floorboard in your room. You'll contact Pinkerton to retrieve it later. You and Joe sneak out the back of the hotel and quietly find your way to the barn where the horses are kept. You cough heavily as you try to get on a horse.

"Are you all right?" Joe asks.

"I can make it. Let's go!"

You ride into the darkness, hoping to reach **28** Maryland before daybreak. Thinking about how lucky you are not to have been caught, you decide your days as a spy in Richmond are over.

THE
–END–

To follow another path, turn to page 11.
To read the conclusion, turn to page 101.

"I think I'm too sick to go," you say. You write a letter for Joe to give to your contacts so they will trust him.

Two days later, you hear bad news—the Confederates caught Joe before he reached Maryland. The next day there's a knock on your door. You open it and a Confederate officer you don't know is standing outside. He arrests you for spying on the Confederacy.

You spend a night in jail before the police take you to the courthouse. Standing there is Joe. To your horror, he describes all your activities as a spy! You realize this man you trusted is trying to save his own life by turning you in.

29

TURN THE PAGE.

When the trial is over, you hear the verdict: guilty! The judge sentences you to death by hanging. Still coughing, you shake as you approach the judge.

"At least let me die like a soldier, with a firing squad," you plead. "Hanging is the death of a common criminal."

"You're no soldier," the judge barks, "so you will hang."

You spend your last week in a jail cell, overcome with cough and fever. The morning of the hanging, you slowly crawl up the gallows. You feel the rope tighten around your neck. It's the last thing you will ever feel.

THE
–END–

To follow another path, turn to page 11.
To read the conclusion, turn to page 101.

"You know I support the South," you tell Johnson. "But that kind of work is too dangerous for a simple businessman like me."

Johnson accepts your answer, and you continue north. You go to Washington to give Pinkerton the information you've gathered. Then you stop in Baltimore before returning south. You see some Knights of Liberty who haven't yet been arrested. You meet them late one November night at a local hotel.

Shortly after midnight, you hear noise outside. You go to the window and see a large number of Union soldiers surrounding the hotel. They burst into the room, grabbing you and other men.

31

"What's going on?" you demand.

TURN THE PAGE.

"We know you're all spying for the South," one officer says. "You're going to jail."

At the jail you learn that Deputy Provost-marshal James McPhail was in charge of the raid. You know that McPhail knows Pinkerton. You ask another officer to send a message to McPhail. "Tell him to contact Mr. Pinkerton and ask if Jacob Smith is all right."

Most Union soldiers were less than 30 years old. Some buglers and drummers were as young as 12.

The officer agrees. That night several officers take you from the jail and put you in a wagon. "As we leave the city," an officer whispers, "jump from the wagon and go back to your rebel friends."

You realize Pinkerton got your message and arranged your escape! You jump from the wagon and run to William Cooper's home. He and the others are impressed with your daring escape— and you have not blown your cover of being a Confederate supporter. But the close call scared you. You don't want to continue spying. You decide to return to Washington and try to help the Union in other ways.

33

THE
-END-

To follow another path, turn to page 11.
To read the conclusion, turn to page 101.

The next day you tell your Memphis friends that you have business in Kentucky. It's a slave state that hasn't left the Union. But Kentuckians have strong feelings both for and against slavery. No one in Memphis will question you traveling to a slave state that is not openly supporting the Union.

Your train arrives in Bowling Green, Kentucky, the next day. You realize right away how split the city's residents are on the subject. Union supporters control the state legislature. In the streets you hear Confederate supporters say, "We should create our own government. Then we can fight for our right to keep slaves." You get plenty of information in Kentucky to send to Pinkerton.

One day you receive a telegram from Pinkerton. "Send peaches home." The message is a code. "Peaches" is the name Pinkerton uses for you. The message means he has a more important job for you in Washington or Maryland. You board a train and head east, ready for your next secret mission.

During the Civil War, slaves did anything they could to escape from slave states such as Kentucky. Those that escaped traveled in wagons or even on foot to reach Union territory.

**THE
-END-**

To follow another path, turn to page 11.
To read the conclusion, turn to page 101.

The two men seem surprised as you walk toward them. "Gentlemen," you say with all your courage. "Do you want something from me?"

"What do you mean?" mumbles the man in the hat.

"I don't know why, but you are clearly following me. I have done nothing wrong."

"No?" the other asks. "What were you doing out at that camp yesterday with Dr. Burns?"

"He wanted me to meet some fine Confederate officers," you reply. "It was my honor, given that I support the Southern cause."

The man in the hat stands and puts his face close to yours. "You sure you weren't trying to get information to send north? You sure you aren't a spy?"

Your heart pounds, but you speak slowly and calmly. "Sir, I am not a spy for anyone."

Now the other man rises, pointing a gun at you. "Well then, you won't mind if we take you back to Memphis and find out."

Suddenly the train lurches as it goes around a wide turn. The men lose their balance, but you're able to bolt past them to the platform outside the car. As the train sways, you leap from the platform and land in the grass by the tracks. Bam! You feel a sharp, stabbing pain in your back. You've been shot! You gasp for breath as the life slowly ebbs out of you.

37

THE
-END-

To follow another path, turn to page 11.
To read the conclusion, turn to page 101.

"Humboldt!" the conductor shouts. You get off at the station. The two men are leaving the train's rear car. You duck behind a large stack of baggage on the station platform. The men don't see you as they pass by. After a moment, you hear one of them say, "I lost him."

"Me too," the other replies. "You go that way, along the tracks. I'll check the station."

You wait a few minutes after the men leave. Then you look out from the pile of baggage and sigh with relief. The men are gone.

A conductor walks by you. "Excuse me—is there a train going to Louisville, Kentucky?" you ask him.

The conductor glances at his pocket watch. "Yes, there's one leaving just now." You thank him and jump aboard. You don't see either man as the train pulls out of the station. You're safe—for now. But as long as you're a spy, you'll live with danger every day.

THE
-END-

To follow another path, turn to page 11.
To read the conclusion, turn to page 101.

Virginian Belle Boyd became a Confederate spy when she was 17. She smuggled information to Southern generals

CHAPTER 3

TRUE TO THE SOUTH

Ever since the war began, you have had mixed feelings. Some of your family members still live and own slaves in your home state of Virginia. You left at age 18 to become an actress. A few years later you married a Northern businessman and moved with him to Washington, D.C. His company did business with the U.S. government. Your husband died before the war, leaving you just enough money to support yourself.

You miss your husband, but you're not lonely. Your friends visit you often. But like your husband, most are Northerners.

"You oppose the Confederacy, don't you?" your friend Mary White asks.

TURN THE PAGE.

In your heart, you don't. How can you turn against your home state and your own family? But you don't want your friends to know that.

You sigh, "I just hate to think of all those young American boys killing one another."

One weekend you have a party. Robert Bradley, one of your husband's old clients, is there. He asks what you think about the war.

"The Southern states can't afford to lose their slaves," you say. "I understand why they wanted to secede. And the states should have the right to make their own laws."

42

"You're from Virginia, aren't you?" Robert asks. You nod. He whispers, "Me too. And like you, I understand why the South is trying to gain its independence." Robert asks if he can return later to discuss something important with you.

Robert calls on you the next day. He says, "You cannot repeat what I am about to tell you. I am secretly working for the Confederacy."

"You're a spy?" you gasp.

"Yes, and I need your help," he says. "You know important businessmen and government officials. You can get information from them."

"I'll do it!" you say. "I am still a Southerner at heart."

Robert teaches you to use a device called a cipher to write coded messages. The cipher has a small and a large wheel, with the small wheel fixed on top of the larger one. On each wheel the alphabet is printed clockwise. By turning the top wheel, you can substitute one letter for another in your messages. Robert also tells you to have more parties, so you'll have a chance to talk to people.

43

TURN THE PAGE.

"Try to meet some military officers too," he suggests. "After a few hours of conversation, they might let some useful information slip."

You have a party each Saturday for several weeks. Some guests talk about where Union troops might be fighting next. You write down what you hear and send the coded messages to Robert. Soon he comes to visit you again.

"I need more help," he says. "We need money to buy supplies for Confederate troops."

Your husband's money is slowly running out. You don't know if you can afford to help. But the soldiers badly need supplies.

44

TO SAY NO, GO TO PAGE 45.

TO SAY YES, TURN TO PAGE 51.

You explain your financial situation. "Is there something else I can do?" you ask.

"Perhaps we can use your home as a safe house for other spies," Robert says. He explains that suspected spies sometimes need a hiding place before they can escape to Virginia. You agree.

"And you must know trustworthy Southerners here in Washington," he says. "Maybe you can recruit them to work for you."

You do know people who can help. Soon you have several other spies working for you. Robert leaves Washington on business. While he is gone, you send messages to another Confederate contact, James Colwell. He is part of the "Secret Line," the network of agents and messengers who send information from Washington to the South.

TURN THE PAGE.

Your freed black servant Abby carries messages to Colwell inside a basket of eggs. You punch a small hole in one egg with a needle and carefully blow out the yolk and white. You then slip the message inside the hollow egg. Even though your actions are helping the Confederacy, Abby remains loyal to you and does as you ask.

When Robert returns, he asks another favor. He wants you to visit captured rebel soldiers as they march to prison camps outside Washington.

"Perhaps you can help some escape," he says. "Or at least get information they might have learned about the Union army."

Helping prisoners escape sounds risky. But you hate the idea of young Southern boys suffering in a Union prison.

TO SAY NO, GO TO PAGE 47.

TO MEET WITH PRISONERS, TURN TO PAGE 48.

Washington is full of Union forts recently built to defend the city. You offer instead to gather information about the forts. Robert nods.

"No one will think such a respectable woman is spying," he says. He asks you to learn the number of guns and the amount of supplies at each fort. You also continue to hold parties and meet with Union officers.

One day Bradley sends you a coded message. You use your cipher to read, "Pinkerton agents watching me closely. May know that you and I are in contact. Be careful!"

Allan Pinkerton runs a detective agency in Chicago. Now he and his men are hunting Confederate spies. You're in danger. Maybe you could still be useful if you left Washington.

TO LEAVE WASHINGTON, TURN TO PAGE 59.

TO KEEP SPYING IN WASHINGTON, TURN TO PAGE 62.

Within a week, Robert tells you that
Confederate prisoners will be passing through
Washington to Baltimore's Fort McHenry. You
prepare food to take to the men.

A Union officer stops you as you approach the
fort. "What is your business here?" he asks.

"I have food for the prisoners. I am just
doing my duty as a Christian," you say with your
friendliest smile.

The officer allows you to bring food to some
of the men. As you greet them, you whisper that
you support the Confederacy. You ask them for
any useful information. That night you use the
cipher to code a message for Robert.

You look for new ways to get information. At one of your parties, a Union government official named Matthew Hansen is very friendly to you. You invite him to come over for tea. He eagerly accepts your invitation.

Some Confederate prisoners of war were sent to camps in Northern states, such as New York.

TURN THE PAGE.

During this and other visits, you act as if you find Matthew and his work fascinating. "The war is dreadful," you say during one visit, "but I am so curious about it. My friend Mary's son is fighting under General Patterson. She says it is so hard to find out what's really happening to the soldiers."

"Well, ma'am, I do know something about our war plans," Hansen said. "As you know, I work for a very important senator."

Matthew begins to describe the plans for an attack in Virginia. After he leaves, you realize you must get the information to Confederate leaders. But Robert is out of town. You could send Abby to Virginia with the message. But this is the most important information you've found. Perhaps you should take it yourself.

50

TO GIVE THE MESSAGE TO ABBY, TURN TO PAGE 55.

TO GO YOURSELF, TURN TO PAGE 57.

"I don't have much money left," you tell him. "But I'll do what I can."

You give Robert the money you have on hand. Afterward you visit the bank and withdraw more money. Instead of giving it to Robert, you decide to buy supplies yourself. One of your husband's old business contacts, Abe Garrett, sells medical supplies. Your black servant Charlie drives your carriage to Garrett's warehouse.

"Why do you need medical supplies?" Garrett asks.

"I know Union hospitals are in need," you say. "I want to donate these to the U.S. Sanitary Commission." Civilians run this commission, which relies on donations to help Union soldiers.

51

"That's very generous," Garrett says. You thank him and smile.

TURN THE PAGE.

That night you tell Charlie to prepare the horse and carriage again.

"We're taking these supplies to Virginia," you say. Charlie looks upset. "What's wrong?" you ask.

"Ma'am, I know you came from Virginia," Charlie says. "And you want to help your family there. But I have family there too. They're still slaves. I'm lucky my old master gave me my freedom. But if the South wins this war, my aunts and uncles and cousins will never be free."

52

Charlie's story touches you. But to you the war isn't about one or two slaves and their freedom. It's about Southern states protecting their rights under the Constitution. Should you deliver the supplies alone or give up your plan?

TO GO TO VIRGINIA, GO TO PAGE 53.

TO STAY IN WASHINGTON, TURN TO PAGE 64.

"I'll go alone," you tell Charlie. "But I have to take these supplies to Virginia."

"Ma'am, it's not safe for you to travel by yourself," he sighs. "I'll go."

You ride through the quiet Washington streets. In the moonlight, you see the U.S. Capitol. Workers are building a larger metal dome for its top. You pass Union forts built on what were farms and orchards just months ago.

The U.S. Capitol's cast iron dome was under construction from 1855 to 1866.

TURN THE PAGE.

You arranged in advance to meet a Confederate supporter named Richard Wallace at the Potomac River. Wallace has a boat and ferries you and Charlie across the river with the supplies. On the other side, you meet Wallace's friend, Arthur. He gives you a carriage and horse to travel to Virginia.

As you near the Virginia border, you see Union soldiers. They signal for you to stop.

"What should we do?" Charlie asks.

TO TURN BACK,
TURN TO PAGE 65.

TO KEEP GOING, TURN TO PAGE 67.

Abby is in the kitchen. You tell her, "I want you to take this message, like you did before."

"Should I get some eggs?" Abby asks.

"No, we don't have time to hollow out an egg. I'm just going to fold it very small and put it in your hair."

Abby stands silently as you place the message inside her hair. Usually it only takes her a few hours to reach one of Robert's contacts.

That night you pace the floor as you wait for Abby to return. As the sky starts to lighten, she is still gone. Around 10:00 a.m., there's a knock at the door. Abby is there—surrounded by Union soldiers!

"Is this your servant?" a soldier asks.

TURN THE PAGE.

You realize Abby has been caught. "No, she is not," you lie. You start to close the door. One of the soldiers steps in. He says, "When we caught her with this message, she said she works for you. And that you gave her the message."

"I'm sorry, ma'am," Abby says as she begins to cry. "I was so scared."

You lower your head as the soldier grabs your arm. You know your next stop is Old Capitol Prison, where the Union holds Confederate supporters and spies. A drafty cell and moldy food await you. You hope you'll survive until the end of the war.

56

THE
-END-

To follow another path, turn to page 11.
To read the conclusion, turn to page 101.

You hire a carriage to take you out of the city. You then begin walking to Virginia. You ask a farmer to direct you to the nearest Confederate camp. He tells you but adds, "I hear there are Northern troops close by. You could get caught."

You don't like the idea of going to prison, but you've known all along that spying was dangerous. "I have to get this information to General Lee," you say.

As you approach the camp, you hear gunfire. Terrified, you run toward a Confederate soldier on horseback. Bullets whiz by as he pulls you up onto the horse. The horse races back to camp, dodging bullets all the way. You give an officer the plans you received from Matthew Hansen.

57

TURN THE PAGE.

"I'll get this information to General Lee right away," the officer says. "Thank you for your bravery."

His praise warms your heart. It's good to know you've done your part for the Confederate cause. But you're finished spying. You'll support the Confederacy in less dangerous ways until the war's end.

As the war dragged on, food shortages became a major problem for Southern civilians. These Southerners are applying for food at a Union camp.

THE
-END-

To follow another path, turn to page 11.
To read the conclusion, turn to page 101.

You still have your makeup and costumes from your actress days. You'll disguise yourself to enter a Union camp in Virginia. You'll pretend to be a young male slave who wants to help the North.

You spend several days getting ready. You cut your long hair very short and buy a black, curly wig. You alter some of your husband's old clothes to fit you. Finally, you put the chemical silver nitrate on your skin to darken it. Late one night you slip out of Washington and cross over into Virginia.

After walking for several days, you come to a Union camp in the Shenandoah Valley. The Union troops are trying to move south toward Richmond. A guard stops you at the edge of the camp.

TURN THE PAGE.

"What are you doing out here?" he asks.

You tell him you're a runaway slave. "All I want to do is help you Yanks beat those rebels," you say, deepening your voice to sound like a young man.

The guard lets you enter the camp. The Union soldiers agree to let you stay with them in exchange for work. You carry food to soldiers and move supplies. You also wander around the camp and listen to the soldiers talk.

The next day a Union officer approaches you. "You say you're a runaway from near here?" he asks.

You can tell he's suspicious. Maybe some of the other runaways in the camp sense you're not really one of them. You just nod. Then the officer reaches toward you. Before you can react, he pulls off your wig!

"Guards!" the officer shouts. "Arrest this boy. Or should I say, this spy."

You're quickly locked in chains. If you're found guilty of spying, you could be hanged. But as the day goes on, you hear cannon fire. The Confederate army is attacking the camp. Waves of blue-coated Union soldiers head out to fight, but they retreat a short time later. The Southern troops quickly overrun the camp.

"Help!" you scream. "I'm a loyal Confederate woman!" A Southern soldier comes over. At first he doesn't believe you're a white woman, but you convince him. He frees you from your chains.

61

"Thank you," you whisper, tears rolling down your cheeks. You decide your days as a spy are over, but at least you're alive.

THE
-END-

To follow another path, turn to page 11.
To read the conclusion, turn to page 101.

A Union government official, Isaac McGee, is scheduled to come to your house that afternoon for tea. You're worried Pinkerton agents are watching you, but you decide to behave as if nothing is wrong and keep the appointment.

Many female Civil War spies were able to gain access or information because men were less likely to suspect a woman of spying. This woman is visiting officers at a Union Army camp in Virginia.

McGee comes and goes without anyone seeing him—or so you think. The next day, you learn McGee was arrested! You know Pinkerton's men assume McGee passed you information. In a panic, you gather the letters you received from Robert Bradley and other Confederate spies. You need to burn them. But before you reach the fireplace, there's a loud knock on your door. You freeze. After another knock, you hear men pushing against the door. You need to run, but your fear won't allow your feet to move.

With a crash, the door breaks open. Three men enter. They grab the papers from your hand.

"You're under arrest for treason," one of them says. You know you'll be spending the rest of the war in a Union prison.

**THE
-END-**

To follow another path, turn to page 11.
To read the conclusion, turn to page 101.

"Charlie, I'm sorry about your family," you say. "I won't take the supplies to Virginia."

The next day you donate the supplies to the Sanitary Commission. Then you gather Charlie and your other black servants into the living room.

"I've decided I don't want to stay in Washington," you tell them. "I'm going back to Virginia."

Your servants look surprised and worried. But they smile when you give them each a little money and say you'll help them find new jobs. You don't know how long the war will last, and there will be more fighting in Virginia. But you want to be with Southerners who know how important it is for the South to win the war.

THE
-END-

To follow another path, turn to page 11.
To read the conclusion, turn to page 101.

As Charlie turns the wagon around, several soldiers approach from the other direction. They also signal you to stop.

"Awfully late to be out, ma'am," one says.

"I couldn't sleep," you reply calmly.

Charlie squirms a bit in his seat.

"I'm sure you won't mind if we take a look in your carriage," says the soldier.

Your heart is racing as fear floods your body. You signal Charlie with your hand to drive away. You make it past the soldiers, but they pull out their guns and fire two warning shots.

65

It doesn't make sense to risk both of your lives. "Stop!" you yell. Charlie pulls up on the horse's reins. The soldiers rush over and look in back, finding the supplies.

TURN THE PAGE.

"Just out for a ride?" the soldiers asks. "I think you were planning on taking these to Virginia."

You are taken to the nearest fort and guarded throughout the night. The next day an officer arrives.

"We searched your house," he says. "We know all about your spying. You'll be deported to the Confederacy. If you come north again, we'll throw you in prison."

Later that day a wagon carries you to Virginia. Charlie remains with the soldiers. He will help with cooking and moving supplies. You know things could have turned out much worse for you. And maybe you'll try to return north to help the Confederacy again. You'd sooner face arrest than have the Union win the war.

THE
-END-

To follow another path, turn to page 11.
To read the conclusion, turn to page 101.

Charlie pulls over toward the soldiers.

"Where are you headed so late?" one asks.

"Oh, sir," you say, beginning to cry. "My mother lives on a farm near here and she's deathly ill. My brother sent word earlier tonight. I must see her!"

"Sorry to hear that, ma'am," he says. "I hope everything turns out all right."

You smile as the carriage rolls on. In Virginia you find a Confederate camp and deliver your supplies. An officer, Colonel Harris, hears your story of how you tricked the Union soldiers. Impressed with your bravery, Harris asks if you'd like to meet President Davis. You agree and soon find yourself on the road to Richmond.

67

You meet Jefferson Davis at the White House of the Confederacy. He greets you warmly and says he is impressed with your service.

TURN THE PAGE.

A few minutes later Davis asks a favor. "Would you help our cause in Europe?" he says. "I need someone to find us money and support."

"I would be honored!" you reply.

In Europe you meet several foreign leaders. They are friendly, but unwilling to give money to the South. On the return journey, your ship runs into a terrible storm. After running aground on a sandbar, the captain orders everyone to abandon ship. Everyone makes their way into lifeboats, and soon you've left the ship behind.

You cling to your lifeboat, which lurches in the rough water. Just then, a wave turns over your boat. You gasp as you land in the freezing water. You struggle for only a few seconds before slipping underneath the water's surface.

THE
-END-

To follow another path, turn to page 11.
To read the conclusion, turn to page 101.

Sarah Emma Edmonds disguised herself as a man to serve as a Union soldier. She also spied on Confederates using different disguises, including by dyeing her skin and pretending to be a male slave.

William Jackson was a slave in Confederate president Jefferson Davis' home. He was also a spy for the Union. Jackson provided high-level information about Confederate strategy and troop movements to the North.

CHAPTER 4

FROM SLAVE TO SPY

The judge glares at you. "The fine is $10 for returning to Virginia. Can you pay it?"

"No, sir," you tell him. You are a free black man who was once a slave here in Richmond, Virginia. Several years ago, your owner, Ellen Lewis, freed you. She then paid for your education in Philadelphia, Pennsylvania. When you returned, you broke a Virginia law that says freed slaves can't remain in the state. Ten dollars is a large amount of money. It would take you years to save that much.

"I can pay it," a woman's voice says behind you. It's Miss Lewis!

71

TURN THE PAGE.

Although Miss Lewis lives in the Confederate capital, she opposes slavery and supports the North. But she surprises you when she tells the judge, "This is all a mistake. He was never freed. He's still my slave."

Outside the courthouse, you shake a bit as you ask Miss Lewis, "Is it true? Am I still your slave?"

"Of course not," she says with a smile. "But it will be much easier to do what I plan if you pretend you are."

You're thankful you are a free man, but you wonder about this plan.

"I am going to tell you something very important," Miss Lewis says. "I am spying for the North."

"Spying?" you ask in disbelief.

Miss Lewis explains how she visits captured Northern soldiers and gathers information from them. Then her servants carry the information on messages written with invisible ink. You've never heard of that before. She explains that she uses a special colorless fluid that becomes visible when it's dipped in milk.

"Will you help me? Miss Lewis asks.

"I would do anything for you," you say.

"Good. I have two missions. You can pose as the slave of a white spy working here. Or we can try to get you a job working for Jefferson Davis."

73

You know working for Davis, the president of the Confederacy, would be risky. But you could get very useful information at his house. The other job might be safer but not as exciting.

TO WORK FOR DAVIS, TURN TO PAGE 74.

TO WORK FOR THE WHITE SPY, TURN TO PAGE 79.

Miss Lewis knows some women who are friendly with Varina Davis, the president's wife.

"I'm going to arrange to have you work as a butler at a party at the Davis house," she explains. "When you show them how well you work, I'm hoping they'll hire you full time."

Miss Lewis' plan works perfectly. Within several weeks you join the staff of slaves at the Davis house. You call yourself Henry and pretend to be not as smart as you really are. Most Southern slaves are not educated, like you are. Since Davis assumes you can't read, he doesn't worry about leaving important documents around the house.

Life for most slaves in Richmond has grown worse since the war started. Before the war slaves didn't always live with their masters. They also had some freedom to travel on their own. But now slaves must live with their owners. They must also have passes to move about the city.

At least your new "master" has a nice home. The president's house has three floors and a basement with a kitchen used to keep food warm. Rooms in the basement are set aside for you and the other servants. Confederate military officers and political leaders often visit. You listen carefully when they talk about the war.

Despite the limits on most slaves' movement, you are able to get out and meet other slaves. You ask them for information they hear about the war. Most are eager to help. They want the North to win, so they can finally earn their freedom.

TURN THE PAGE.

You don't see Miss Lewis often. But she is part of a network of spies working in Richmond. You give information to Tom McNiven. He works as a baker and delivers bread to Richmond homes. When he comes to the Davis' house, you report the information you've gathered. Your sharp memory serves you well. It would be too risky to write things down, since you're not supposed to know how to write.

One morning, Tom has a question for you. "Would you like to do more to gather information? We want someone to join the Legal League and recruit more spies."

76 He explains the Legal League is a secret group of blacks who support legally ending slavery. You like the idea of recruiting more spies, but you worry that doing this may put you at greater risk of being exposed as a spy yourself.

TO SAY NO, GO TO PAGE 77.

TO JOIN THE LEGAL LEAGUE, TURN TO PAGE 87.

"Sorry, Tom," you tell him. "I have all I can handle working at the Davis house."

One day Davis enters his library with several men. You try to listen to their conversation outside the door, but nothing is clear. After a few hours, the men leave.

You start to enter the library. "I just wanted to clean up a bit, sir," you tell Davis.

Jefferson Davis was the only president of the Confederacy. He held the office from 1861 to 1865.

TURN THE PAGE.

"Not now, Henry," Davis says. "I have important work to do."

You're more curious than ever about what Davis was talking about with the men. Finally he leaves the room and tells you to clean up.

You rush over to a stack of documents on a table. Some describe a new cannon the Confederacy is developing. There are drawings and a description about how far it can shoot. You don't know much about weapons, but you realize this gun could be harmful to Union soldiers.

78

There's too much information to memorize it all. You could try to memorize a few pages now and come back later. But Davis could lock the papers away before you have a chance to come back. Maybe you should take them all to Miss Lewis' house.

TO LEAVE WITH THE PAPERS, TURN TO PAGE 89.

TO READ SOME NOW AND SOME LATER, TURN TO PAGE 91.

You know about Allan Pinkerton and his detectives. They spy for the Union and try to catch spies working in the North. Miss Lewis takes you to meet a Pinkerton agent in Richmond, George O'Leary. With him is Sally Lawton, who is also a spy. Lawton and O'Leary are pretending to be a married couple from Baltimore who support the South.

"What should I do?" you ask O'Leary.

"In public, you'll act as our servant," he says. "Whenever you can, go out and talk to the city's slaves. Some of them work for government leaders and military officers. They might have useful information."

The next day you spend several hours meeting slaves in the city. One of them, Jenny, works for President Jefferson Davis.

79

TURN THE PAGE.

"I hear him talking with generals about who's going where next," Jenny tells you.

"Can you write down what you learn and send me a message?" you ask.

"I never learned to write," Jenny says. "And they don't let me out of the house much."

"Maybe we can use a code," you say. You come up with a plan for Jenny to signal you using clothes she hangs outside on a clothesline. Specific shirts or blankets represent the main Confederate generals. When she moves that shirt or blanket from one end of the line to the other, that means that the general is moving in that direction.

Over the next few weeks, the code works perfectly. You give Jenny's information to O'Leary.

You like working as a spy, but you think there is more you can do to help the North. O'Leary understands.

"There are Northern black soldiers fighting for the Union now," he tells you. "And President Lincoln freed the slaves in the South with the Emancipation Proclamation. Some in South Carolina left their masters and are fighting too. Others serve as spies and scouts."

You lived in South Carolina as a boy, before you were sold to Miss Lewis' family. It might be good to go back.

"Or you could help Union troops fighting in Virginia," O'Leary says. "They rely on information from blacks who know the countryside."

TO GO TO SOUTH CAROLINA, TURN TO PAGE 82.

TO STAY IN VIRGINIA, TURN TO PAGE 84.

O'Leary writes a note giving you permission as his slave to travel to visit relatives in South Carolina. But to be safe, you travel mostly at night and stay away from large towns.

Along the way you meet several runaway slaves seeking the safety of Union military camps. They plan to volunteer to fight for the Union.

"They've got black soldiers there," one runaway says. "Harriet Tubman is their leader."

You know that name. Some people call her Moses, because she has helped so many slaves reach the North and gain their freedom. In the Bible, Moses helped the Jewish people of ancient Israel gain their freedom from slavery.

You wish the men good luck as they head north. Now you're determined to reach Tubman and the army with which she is traveling.

A few days later you reach the Second South Carolina Volunteers camp. It has about 300 blacks, although some white soldiers are there too. While a white officer leads the blacks, Harriet Tubman is playing an important role for the unit. You ask to meet her.

Harriet is a sturdy woman with a large scar on her forehead. She says, "I have scouts all up and down the rivers here, looking for Confederate forces. Would you like to join them?"

Both scouts and spies work behind enemy lines. You like the idea of working for the famous Harriet Tubman. But you came to South Carolina to help and maybe fight alongside the black soldiers.

83

TO BECOME A SCOUT, TURN TO PAGE 94.

TO STAY WITH THE TROOPS, TURN TO PAGE 96.

You set out from Richmond and head north. The main Union army in Virginia is based near the town of Warrenton. Along the way you note any Confederate forts or army camps. You can give this information to the Union forces.

You come upon a group of Union scouts. Like spies, they work behind enemy lines to gather information. But since they are soldiers, they don't face execution if they are caught. Instead they are usually treated as prisoners of war. You tell them about working as a spy in Richmond. The officer in charge, Captain Will Carson, is impressed.

"You should travel with us," Carson says. "You can go into towns that we can't. People will think you're a new slave from a nearby plantation."

You travel the countryside looking for Confederate troops. At times you meet runaway slaves who have information about the troops. You send this information back to the army in Warrenton in coded messages.

One night as you return to your camp in the woods, you hear a gunshot.

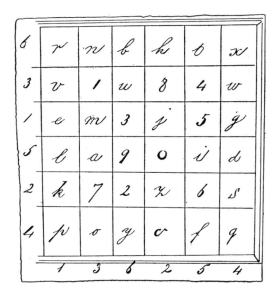

Civil War spies used various cipher code sheets or disks to create secret messages to transfer information.

TURN THE PAGE.

"Get down!" Carson orders. You and the other scouts obey. Back in Richmond, you never had to worry about getting shot. But you are in enemy territory. Confederate troops patrol the area.

You hear a few more shots. Then they stop.

"There must be only a few of them," Carson says. He points to some large trees nearby. "If we can get behind them, we can return fire."

Carson motions to the other scouts to get up. As you all run for the trees, more shots ring out. Carson screams and falls to the ground. You run to him.

86

"Keep running!" Carson orders you, grimacing in pain. "I'll make it."

You want to run for cover. But how can you leave Carson here alone?

TO HELP CARSON, TURN TO PAGE 97.

TO RUN, TURN TO PAGE 98.

"I'll do anything to help the Union," you tell Tom. Tom arranges for you to meet another black spy, Stephen Wright. He is pretending to be the servant of a white spy. The spy works for Allan Pinkerton, who's in charge of many Northern spies working in the South.

That Sunday you steal away from your duties to meet Stephen. He tells you to meet him and the rest of the group at a local church the following Sunday. "At the door of the meeting room, give this password: 'For light and liberty,'" Stephen says.

The next Sunday, you go to the church. As the service goes on, Stephen gets up and goes to a back room. You follow him and give the password to a man standing at the door. Inside, five men are sitting around a table.

TURN THE PAGE.

"This is our newest member," Stephen says. You listen as the group shares information they've heard over the past few weeks. One has been working on a ship and describes Confederate shore defenses. Another ran away from his master and knows where troops are heading next.

Suddenly, you hear shouts. You all leap to your feet. But before you can do anything, someone pounds on the door.

"Open up!" a voice yells. "We know what you slaves are doing in there."

You don't have to open the door to know who it is. Someone has told the police about the Legal League. When they come in, they'll take you to jail. You hope your job with Davis will spare you a beating. But your days as a spy are over.

THE
-END-

To follow another path, turn to page 11.
To read the conclusion, turn to page 101.

88

You gather the papers and peek out the doorway. No one is around. The library is on the first floor, so you have a good chance of reaching the front door unseen. You take a deep breath before walking to the front door. Once outside, you try to walk as if you're just running an errand.

Miss Lewis' servant lets you in. When Miss Lewis enters, she says, "What are you doing here?"

"I had to show you these," you say, handing her the papers. "If I'm right, President Lincoln and his generals will want to know about this."

Miss Lewis looks at the papers and quickly nods in agreement with you—this new weapon could be disastrous.

TURN THE PAGE.

"With these plans, the Union army can now make its own cannon." She shakes your hand. "Good work."

Miss Lewis copies the plans, so you can sneak the originals back into the Davis house. You're pleased that your brave actions may help the North win the war and end slavery.

Jefferson Davis' house was also called the White House of the Confederacy.

THE
-END-

To follow another path, turn to page 11.
To read the conclusion, turn to page 101.

You try to memorize the first few pages. But you hear footsteps in the hall. You put down the papers and pick up the plates and cups the guests left behind.

President Davis enters. "Thank you, Henry. You can leave now."

"Yes sir," you say.

The next day, Tom comes for his bread delivery. You tell him about the cannon.

"I'll pass the information on to Pinkerton," he says. "But you might not have time to look at the rest. There's talk on the street that Mrs. Davis doesn't trust one of her servants," he says. "She thinks there may be a spy in the house."

Your heart sinks. "Does she think it's me?" you ask.

TURN THE PAGE.

"We don't know. But if they do, you won't be safe anywhere in Virginia. You need to get up north as quickly as possible."

To escape, you need to create a distraction. That night President Davis has a party. You're sent several times to the basement kitchen to get food and drinks. Each time you place sticks of wood together in the corner of the basement. Around 10 p.m., you toss a lit match on the wood and go upstairs. A few minutes later, someone notices smoke and yells "Fire!"

People flee the house, including President Davis and his family. You slip out of the house and head to Miss Lewis'. You tell her about the fire and why you set it.

"You can't stay here," she says. "They might come to question me, since they know I hate the Confederacy. I know a safe house where you can spend the night. Tomorrow we'll make sure you get out of Virginia."

Your spying days are over, but you can still help the Union. The Union army is now accepting black soldiers. You decide to go back to Philadelphia and enlist. That way you can keep fighting to end slavery.

THE
-END-

To follow another path, turn to page 11.
To read the conclusion, turn to page 101.

You set off in small boat up the Combahee River on June 2, 1863. You travel with a black scout, Walter Plowden. Unlike most of the other scouts, he's served with the Union army since the beginning of the war. For a time he worked in a military hospital. "But when I had the chance to work for our Moses," he said, "I jumped at it."

You sail the boat up the river just before daybreak. You need some light so you can spot Confederate torpedoes in the water. You note their positions so you can later safely guide Union ships up the river.

The next morning you and the other scouts lead the Union boats. Tubman had already arranged for runaway slaves to meet the boats at certain spots along the river. The plan is to take as many slaves as possible back to the Union camps, giving them their freedom.

Scouts Isaac and Samuel Heyward lead the soldiers to the plantation that they escaped from. The plantation's slaves run to the boats near the shore. The soldiers then set the plantation buildings on fire. Soon flames and smoke are all that you can see. Two more plantations meet the same fate by the end of the day.

About 700 slaves escape to freedom during the Combahee raid. Even though you weren't a soldier, you played an important role in the fight to win the war and gain freedom for all black people.

THE
-END-

To follow another path, turn to page 11.
To read the conclusion, turn to page 101.

You stay and train with the black troops. Most escaped from slavery just a few weeks before.

The morning of June 3, 1863, you set out on a raid Tubman helped plan. Her scouts guide Union boats up the Combahee River. You go ashore and begin marching inland. No Confederate troops are in sight. Your group torches the buildings at one plantation before heading back to the river. There you see escaping slaves running to board the Union ships. Altogether, about 700 slaves escape to freedom that day, and two more plantations are burned.

You've traveled far over the last few years. You liked your work as a spy, and you will go back to it. But you're glad you were here to see so many other black people gaining their freedom.

**THE
-END-**

To follow another path, turn to page 11.
To read the conclusion, turn to page 101.

96

There's a pause in the shooting. The Confederate troops must be reloading. You only have a few seconds to act. You rush over to Carson. Blood is streaming from his leg.

"I'm going to carry you," you tell him as you sling his body over your shoulder. As the firing starts again, you run for the trees. One shot whizzes by your head. You hear another make a strange sound. Carson goes limp. You look back, and now blood is flowing from his head. You know he must be dead, but you refuse to put down his body. The scouts can give him a proper burial later. But you won't see it. A bullet goes through your back and pierces your heart. You drop Carson's body as you fall to the ground and quickly die.

97

THE
-END-

To follow another path, turn to page 11.
To read the conclusion, turn to page 101.

You tremble as you run. The scouts shoot back at the soldiers. Smoke hovers around you. Through it, you see Carson trying to crawl toward the trees. It was a mistake to leave him there. You head back toward him, hoping some of the smoke will hide you from the rebel soldiers.

"What are you doing?" Carson asks as you reach his side. He can barely whisper.

"Coming for you, sir," you say. You help Carson to his feet, and then sling him over your back. You hear him cry in pain as you brush against his injured leg. But carrying him is the only way to reach safety quickly.

98

The other scouts crouch behind a tree. You reach them and put Carson down. You then fall to the ground. You are exhausted, but you are alive. So is Carson. A few seconds later, the Confederate firing stops.

"You held them off," Carson says to the scouts. "Good work." Then he looks at you, holding out his hand. "And you saved my life. Thank you."

You shake his hand. It's one of the few times in your life that a white man has shown his thanks to you. You feel good about showing bravery you didn't know you had.

By the end of the war, black soldiers made up nearly 10 percent of the Union army.

99

THE
-END-

To follow another path, turn to page 11.
To read the conclusion, turn to page 101.

*In addition to working for the Union as a cook and a nurse,
Harriet Tubman became a spy and organizer of raiding partie*

CHAPTER 5

ESPIONAGE HELPS WIN THE WAR

The North won the Civil War in 1865, partly because of information provided by spies. Some information came from Confederate prisoners and deserters. Southern blacks who ran to Union lines also provided key information. But Union military leaders also received useful information from their trained scouts and Southerners who opposed secession.

During the war the North also established the Bureau of Military Information. Its agents studied documents found on the battlefield and even information openly published in Southern newspapers. They wanted to learn what the Confederates might do next.

The Union also used new methods to gather intelligence, such as putting men inside hot-air balloons and launching them near Confederate camps. Confederates responded by painting logs to look like cannons. Spies in the balloons couldn't get an accurate idea of how many guns they had.

Some details of Civil War spying remain unknown. After the war Union officials or people who ran spy rings destroyed their files. Both sides executed some spies, but we don't know all of their names. They didn't always carry papers that revealed their identity.

Civil War spies used technology such as binoculars, telegraphs, and ciphers for creating coded messages.

Today espionage remains an important way to gather information from possible enemies even before a war starts. Spying remains important during wars too. The United States, along with many other countries, relies on satellites in space to reveal movement of other countries' troops and weapons. The U.S. government also tracks potential enemies by listening in on their phone calls or secretly reading their e-mail.

Spying is about gathering information. High-tech tools help, but governments still rely on human spies. Like during the Civil War, some spies pretend to be someone they are not. And all risk being arrested if they are caught at their job. Spying remains an exciting but dangerous business.

During the Civil War, some men convicted of spying were executed. Scouts and women spies, however, would have been punished less harshly and sent to a prison camp. These Southern prisoners are being held at a Union camp in Indiana.

NOVEMBER 1860—Abraham Lincoln is elected president of the United States.

DECEMBER 1860—South Carolina is the first Southern state to secede from the Union.

JANUARY 1861—Mississippi, Florida, Alabama, Georgia, and Louisiana join South Carolina in seceding. By May, Texas, Virginia, Arkansas, North Carolina, and Tennessee join them.

FEBRUARY 1861—Pinkerton agents sneak Lincoln into Washington D.C., preventing a plot to kill him.

MARCH 4, 1861—Lincoln is sworn in as the United States president.

APRIL 12, 1861—The Civil War begins when Confederate troops fire on Fort Sumter in South Carolina.

JULY 21, 1861—Confederate forces win their first major victory in Virginia at the First Battle of Bull Run.

NOVEMBER 6, 1861—Jefferson Davis is elected president of the Confederate States of America.

SPRING 1862—Fighting occurs in Virginia's Shenandoah Valley.

JANUARY 1, 1863—President Lincoln issues the Emancipation Proclamation, freeing slaves in territory under Confederate control.

JUNE 3, 1863—Harriet Tubman and free blacks take part in the Union's successful Combahee River raid in South Carolina.

APRIL 9, 1865—The Civil War ends as Confederate General Robert E. Lee surrenders to Union General Ulysses S. Grant in Appomattox Court House, Virginia.

OTHER PATHS TO EXPLORE

In this book, you've seen how events from the past look different from three points of view. Perspectives on history are as varied as the people who lived it. Seeing history from many points of view is an important part of understanding it. Here are ideas for other Civil War espionage points of view to explore:

+ The Civil War forced Americans to decide between supporting the Union or the Confederacy. Some people simply decided to support their home state while others made decisions based on their beliefs about slavery. How might a person's individual experiences have influenced his or her actions and perspectives during the war? (Craft and Structure)

+ The Union had far more resources than the Confederacy in most major areas. For example, the Union's population was around twice the size of the Confederacy's population. In what ways might differences in resources have influenced each side's espionage needs and development during the war? Support your answers using information from at least two other texts or valid Internet sources. (Integration of Knowledge and Ideas)

READ MORE

Goodman, Michael E. *Civil War Spies.* Mankato, Minn.: Creative Education, 2015.

Jarrow, Gail. *Lincoln's Flying Spies: Thaddeus Lowe and the Civil War Balloon Corps.* Honesdale, Pa.: Calkins Creek, 2010.

Otfinoski, Steven. *Yankees and Rebels: Stories of U.S. Civil War Leaders.* North Mankato, Minn.: Capstone Press, 2015.

Samuels, Charlie. *Timeline of the Civil War.* New York: Gareth Stevens Pub., 2012.

Sodaro, Craig. *Civil War Spies.* North Mankato, Minn.: Capstone Press, 2014.

INTERNET SITES

FactHound offers a safe, fun way to find Internet sites related to this book. All of the sites on FactHound have been researched by our staff.

Here's all you do:
Visit *www.facthound.com*
Type in this code: 9781491458594

GLOSSARY

cover (KUH-ver)—a fake name or story that a spy uses to stay safe

curfew (KUHR-fyoo)—a time by which people must be off public streets and in their homes

deport (di-PORT)—to send people back to their own country

detective (di-TEK-tiv)—a person who investigates crimes or collects information for people

double agent (DUH-buhl AY-juhnt)—a spy who works for one country's spy agency but is really loyal to another

emancipation (i-MAN-si-pay-shuhn)—freedom from slavery

espionage (ESS-pee-uh-nahzh)—the actions of a spy to gain sensitive national, political, or economic information

intelligence (in-TEL-uh-jenss)—secret information about an enemy's plans or actions

secede (si-SEED)—to formally withdraw from an organization or group, often to form another organization

torpedo (tor-PEE-doh)—an underwater weapon that explodes when it hits a target, such as a ship

treason (TREE-zuhn)—the act of betraying one's country

BIBLIOGRAPHY

Bonansinga, Jay R. *Pinkerton's War: The Civil War's Greatest Spy and the Birth of the U.S. Secret Service.* Guilford, Conn.: Lyons Press, 2012.

Catton, Bruce. *The American Heritage New History of the Civil War.* New York: Viking, 1996.

Clinton, Catherine. *Harriet Tubman: The Road to Freedom.* Boston: Little, Brown, 2004.

Donnelly, Paul. "Harriet Tubman's Great Raid." *The New York Times.* June 7, 2013. http://opinionator.blogs.nytimes.com/2013/06/07/harriet-tubmans-great-raid/?_php=true&_type=blogs&_php=true&_type=blogs&_r=1

Edmonds, S. Emma E. *Nurse and Spy in the Union Army: Comprising the Adventures and Experiences of a Woman in Hospitals, Camps, and Battle-fields.* Hartford, Conn.: Williams, 1865.

Jones, Wilmer L. *Behind Enemy Lines: Civil War Spies, Raiders, and Guerrillas.* Dallas: Taylor Pub. Co., 2001.

Recko, Corey. *A Spy for the Union: The Life and Execution of Timothy Webster.* Jefferson, N.C.: McFarland & Company, Inc., Publishers, 2013.

"Women Spies of the Civil War." *Smithsonian.* May 8, 2011. http://www.smithsonianmag.com/history/women-spies-of-the-civil-war-162202679/?no-ist

INDEX